THE WATER PUZZLE
FACTS ABOUT YOUR **DRINKING WATER**

THE WATER PUZZLE:

FACTS ABOUT YOUR **DRINKING WATER**

by
PHIL RANIERI

Copyright © 2014 by Phil Ranieri.

Library of Congress Control Number:	2014913328
ISBN: Hardcover	978-1-4990-4966-4
Softcover	978-1-4990-4968-8
eBook	978-1-4990-4967-1

All rights reserved. No part of this book may be reproduced or transmitted in any form or by any means, electronic or mechanical, including photocopying, recording, or by any information storage and retrieval system, without permission in writing from the copyright owner.

Any people depicted in stock imagery provided by Thinkstock are models, and such images are being used for illustrative purposes only.
Certain stock imagery © Thinkstock.

This book was printed in the United States of America.

Rev. date: 07/10/2014

To order additional copies of this book, contact:
Xlibris LLC
1-888-795-4274
www.Xlibris.com
Orders@Xlibris.com
649860

Chapter One

It is said that the solution to pollution is dilution. And there is a lot of truth in that statement. Yet it can be said that nothing is 100%!

Drinking water is the most precious of commodities on our plant. Without water we as a people could not exist, crops could not grow, animals could not survive. Everyday thousands of men and women worldwide are working to provide safe drinking water in adequate quantities for the citizens of this plant. In the following chapters I will explain the thought processes behind the treatment of drinking water production, some experiences I have encountered, and concerns in this post 9/11 age.

In the mid-1980's when the U.S. Congress passed the Safe Drinking Water Act, the EPA was entrusted to develop regulations to protect our nations drinking water supplies, protect our citizens from the risk of contaminated waters. But the EPA alone did not have the enforcement capabilities to handle this task, so along came Primacy. Which is each state accepting responsibility to enforce the laws enacted. In order for this to happen each state had to adopt their own laws and regulations to legally take over the reins from the EPA. In turn the EPA offered money to the state agencies involved to run their programs, with the catch that the states had to adopt the EPA mandates or lose monies.

Before all this, some communities had open reservoirs with only Chlorination for disinfection, or wells with no treatment. The quality of such water was not what we would consider good, by today's standards.

One thing to look at as we get into this discussion is the mindset of the EPA and state agencies whose task it is to make sure the water is safe.

To the regulatory community it is not only a matter of actualities, but also one of probabilities. As a regulator, I was involved with a water system which utilized two springs and a well. The water authority used chlorine as its disinfectant, back some years ago when the government agencies had found a little known parasite called Giardia. Well it was found that normal levels of chlorine would not kill that critter. Why, because the organism was encased in a encapsulated sheath. This prevented chlorine from reaching the organism, so no kill rate. The effects of Giardia in humans is, once the organism enters the intestine it attaches to the stomach wall and causes one to feel ill. There are other such organisms which are more deadly than Giardia, such as Cryptosporidium, smaller than Giardia and also encapsulated. A number of deaths occurred in Milwaukee, Wisconsin due to Cryptosporidium. Well EPA and the states developed MPA's or Microscopic Particle Analysis to look for such parasites. In this test anywhere from 300 to 1000 gallons of both raw untreated water and finished water is collected through cloth filters each filter is bagged and sent to a testing lab to be studied. Now back to the water system I referred to, and the government mindset. The results of the MPA was that no Giardia was found, but, other microscopic organisms were found of a size that matched Giardia. So looking at it from a probability standpoint, Giardia could get into the system. As such the Authority was still given the task of a remedy to the situation. Which I am happy to say they came up with the use of slow sand filtration to solve the problem. Now slow sand filtration is a method by which a large sand filter is put in place, and the formation of what is called a schmuttzdeck is formed to trap any and all particles from the water. This takes up more time for the water to travel thru the filter and out to the clearwell. Written in the regulations in many states are provisions for legal recourse on the part of their citizens, an added reason why water companies work hard at providing the safest possible water to their customer base. In order to get a kill of these parasites using chlorine as a combatant, chlorine levels in the vicinity of 2.5 parts per million {ppm} or greater with a contact time of at least twenty minutes or more is required. Now to a person who is sensitive to chlorine they would notice the concentration right away. There are other disinfection devices out there which can do the job, but are not permitted as a sole disinfectant by EPA. Ozone and Ultraviolet light are two. EPA does not approve for sole use as disinfectants one because they do not leave a measured trace in finished water and in the case of UV light which does not work well on viruses. In order for a water system to prove the effectiveness of either, daily bacteria tests would need to be performed. With forty eight hour turn around time and the costs involved this would be impractical. Before I leave this issue for another section of the book, I want to explain about the standard Total Coliform Bacteria test. This is the standard which all states go by. Total Coliform is known as an indicator organism, we have them in our intestines and they are found in soils. To the average person they cause no harm, but, to EPA and the states if you find Total Coliforms in a sample then other organisms might be there too. Again the probabilities, better safe than sorry to EPA and the states. Regulations designed with you in mind, for your well being.

Lets turn our attention to chemical elements in our water and just what effects they have on us. The EPA has put out a list of what they call Primary and Secondary contaminants. As well as VOC AND SOC lists {Volatile Organic Compounds} and {Synthetic Organic Compounds}. These are man made compounds which are considered to be cancer causing agents. Such items as pesticides, herbicides come under the SOC's. Some solvents, cleaning agents, lubricants fit in the VOC category.

Now I want to talk about lead and copper, I had an experience once where the water entering the building in which I worked was aggressive. By aggressive I am referring to the ability of water to act as a solvent. Water at a PH of 7.0 or lower will react over time with soft metals, which is what lead and copper are. Now given time water will work on these soft metals and when a tap is opened out comes water with lead and copper mixed in. Two women came to my office on a Monday {building was closed over weekend} one of the women, had a blue color to her fingernails and the whites of her eyes. Caused by constant drinking of the water with lead deposits. How they discovered the problem was by filling a Styrofoam cup with water from the tap and letting it sit for several minutes a blue green deposit formed on the bottom. To correct this problem the building manager had the lines flushed early Monday mornings before opening the building. Another case involving lead and copper was that of a school building. It seems the water authority supplying water to that school had a hit for lead, from that building. I went to the school and pulled samples, which did show higher lead levels. In the investigation that followed it was found that thr electrical appliances were grounded to the water lines and that was where the problem was. Electrolysis will pull metals out of suspension, this was the case. The school had a new grounding field installed outside of the building and the problem was solved.

Another issue you might hear water plant people talk about is Turbidity, which is cloudiness or a discoloration to the water. Why turbidity is important is that harmful microorganisms could get past the disinfection agent and get out into the system causing people to become ill. Now in a conventional treatment system we should not have this problem because all the dirt particles should have settled out before the water reaches the filters. A conventional system is one that uses Flocculation {mixing the chemicals with the raw water}, Sedimentation holding the water and chemicals in a basin to allow the dirt particles to settle out, Filtration the water travels thru sand and gravel to a drain system. Then into a Clearwell where chlorine is added to kill any organisms which passed thru the filter. This is a simple explanation of the process, but serves the purpose.

Now people these days like to talk about the harmful effects of chlorine on the human body. Well, when you look at the amounts of chlorine in our water supplies, it's not that great. We are talking about parts per million these amounts are so small one would need to drink eight or more glasses a day every day for seventy years before any effects would occur. So you would say well I drink bottled water. Where did this bottled water come from? Usually from a Public Water system, they pull out the chlorine by usually running the water thru Granular Activated Carbon filters, then hit it with Ozone before bottling. The thing about granular activated carbon is its ability to pull chlorine and other elements out of water. Several companies sell these type of filters for home use. But the carbon does get used up and you must replace the filters. Well now if you use the water coolers with the five gallon containers, just how safe are you? When a water bottler sells these five gallon cooler units to homes and to businesses, who knows what these places do with the empties before they get back to the bottler. I had one experience where a family had a cooler, they noticed an odor to the water and called us in. Sure enough there was an odor to the bottle they saved for me. I found the distributor for this product and spoke with the company who bottled the water. I was given the lot number by the bottler and picked up an unopened bottle from the same lot. I sent both the opened and unopened bottles to our lab for testing. Sure enough the unopened bottle was fine, but, the opened bottle had traces of a cleaning solvent. I went back to the bottler with the results, it seems their employee who gives the bottles a sniff test before reuse either had a cold or just missed this container. Now the company has since gone to mechanical air testers to check each bottle for contaminants. But you do not know what a person might use these bottles for. Oh and lest I forget the bottles were cleaned as they were returned to the plant.

Chapter Two

In this chapter I want to talk about Bottled, Vended, and Hauled water for home use. All three are regulated by the EPA/States, and must meet the same standards as all public water suppliers do. In some cases bottled water is just reprocessed water from a public water system. What the bottler does is run the finished water through GAC (Granular Activated Carbon) filters to strip the chlorine, and any other treatment chemicals that might be there out. Then put ozone to the water for disinfection, a requirement of EPA/States. Now ozone is oxygen under electric charge the oxygen turns from O/2 to O/3, a simple explanation of the process. In most states the lead agency for the Safe Drinking Water Act inspects the bottling plant for the gallon sizes and above. Well most bottlers, bottle in a number of sizes, anywhere from 20oz bottles up to five gallon containers, so the inspector sees it all. Under regulations, sampling for these bottlers must be done on a weekly basis for each month, and each week they bottle. Should the bottler not have a bottling run then they would notify the inspector of such. Bottlers are held to much the same standards that the community water systems are held to. With bacteria tests, and in some cases organics, and even radiological, performed to insure the water you buy is safe for consumption. In my past experiences, I have had one bottler that I dealt with on a regular basis. They purchased water from a community system that used large mountain springs for their source. To meet federal requirements, as they called their water spring water. In a later chapter I will go into the relative safety of this type of operation.

Now I want to turn my attention to vended water operations. There are two such types, one for the person who wants to fill a gallon container, and another for bulk use, say a thousand gallons at a time.

The units you find at your local supermarket are for gallon containers and are hooked up to an existing public water line. Inside the unit you will find a GAC filter, to again pull out the chlorine and other chemicals from the treatment process and usually an ultraviolet disinfection unit. The vending machine supplier will come to the store to service the units and to pull the Bacteria samples, usually on a monthly basis. Service usually calls for a check of the carbon filter; some waters will use up a filter faster than others, and will need replacing sooner. And a yearly replacement of the UV light bulb, the UV manufacturer usually calls for yearly replacement of the bulbs, due to a weakening of the bulb. When inspecting these units, I always looked at the cleanliness of the spout. And then I looked at the storage of the containers and their caps. In supermarkets the bottles were usually stored in the back storerooms where dirt and dust would be found. The bottle suppliers would bag them up in large clear plastic bags and supply the caps in a separate bag. The concern here is that dirt or dust would get into the bottles and not be cleaned out, prior to use by the consumer. I have yet to find an illness here, so the stores have been doing their part. One other issue here is where the store keeps the containers stored. Are there any overhead waste lines that might leak onto the bottles? I always made a point of this if found, and would have the store manager store the bottles and caps away from any lines.

Now let's look at bulk vending units, how they work and any problems they might pose. These types of units are coin operated and have a building where a truck with a tank could pull up. A hose is connected and the person getting the water would pull the hose to their tank. Inside the building is the waterline with backflow preventer, and a water meter to check on usage of the unit. I was involved in the construction of one such unit some years back. I would inspect this unit every year, and would look at the hose end for any dirt buildup, or cracks in the hose. When this one unit was ready to go on line, our department engineers and myself went out for the initial inspection. But it seems our regulations did not full cover the hose, as in this case, the hose could reach the ground. Thus the possibility for contamination, this could come back on both the hauling company {if that is who is getting the water}, and the water authority supplying the water. In the case of this vending unit, I had the owner run a cable to a nearby telephone pole and had the hose connected to that cable. So there was no chance that the hose would touch the ground and get contaminated, problem solved.

Now I want to talk about the haulers, and how we look at them.

Haulers have their own trucks, and either gets the water from at the water plant. Or they get the water from remote metered locations, which the water authorities keep track of. In the past fire departments would sometimes, in some areas, go to a hydrant or to the water plant, fill their tanker and supply people who needed water. Now some people had tanks or cisterns to fill, some people just wanted their swimming pools filled. Well states started taking notice of these fire departments, and discouraged this practice as best we could. Reason being, the fire departments sometimes, would fill their tankers out of a nearby creek when fighting a fire. Well one the states did not permit these fire companies under the SDWA, nor did we inspect them. Also just how well they cleaned these tankers out, or did they. And there never was any sampling done on these fire trucks, regulated haulers must sample from each load as part of their permit, sampling again for bacteria.

For years, in many states, the haulers were not permitted. Not until a few years back did this become an issue, and we slowly worked to find and permit haulers. Regular inspections of haulers is a must, things to look at are the insides of the tank for cleanliness, as well as the hoses to make sure no dirt could get into a customer's storage tank.

Chapter Three

In this chapter I want to look contaminants and show how the EPA/States look at them. This chapter will deal with the microbiologicals, and the benchmarks used, as well as their effects on us. The EPA came up with what is referred to as MCL's, or maximum contaminant levels. This is used for as the standard by which all contaminants are measured. Basically, the lower the MCL number the greater the risk to people, higher numbers less risk. Now these numbers have been placed so low that {for chemicals} that it would take years for any effects to be found in people. But now we are looking at microorganisms, this is not the case here. The first one I want to look at is Total Coliform, used as the standard in sampling. It is just the indicator that other organisms could be there, and is not a health threat to humans. I once sampled private homeowners well and found a total coli form count of eighteen, no one was ill from that. But now I want to talk about E. Coli and Fecal Coliform, these are the bad ones. They come from human or animal waste and could be of harm to infants or people with HIV. In some states, when a positive total coli form sample is found the labs will automatically look for fecal coli form. Chlorine disinfection will kill off these organisms, why we require its use, for your protection.

The next one I want to talk about is Cryptosporidium, a very small one that is encased in a sheath; normal levels of chlorine will not touch it. Found in human or animal waste, it will cause diarrhea, vomiting, and cramps. Some deaths have been attributed to this critter, but, you can kill it by boiling the water first, {as with most all microorganisms}.

The next one on my list is Giardia, larger than Cryptosporidium, when ingested it attaches to the wall of the intestine and causes diarrhea, vomiting and cramps. Although this one is a hit and miss organism, one glass of water could be free of, another could have it. Like Cryptosporidium it is encased in a sheath, so normal chlorine does not effect it. There is medication for this, I understand it is nasty tasting, so best not to pick this up.

The next one on my list is Legionella, known to cause a type of pneumonia it is felt that this one is found mostly in heating, air conditioning units, and the water that is used in some units. It is found in water, so it is of concern. Chlorine will kill this one, but, not as much was known about this critter. The next one I want to talk about, while you can kill the organism by boiling, it will still do harm. And that one is Clostridium Perfringens, it is not the kill that is of concern to us. But the toxin produced by the organism, that can hurt you. A toxin is a chemical compound that you cannot get rid of by boiling. So if found in finished water, drink bottled water, you'll be better off, as this toxin can kill you.

There is one microorganism which causes some taste and odor problems in finished water supplies. This group is known as cyano bacteria, the best known of these is blue—green algae. This one causes problems after it dies off during treatment but emitting a compound called geosmin. Algae love warm still waters and sunlight to grow and multiply. Known as blooms, these algae will multiply at such a rate that large thick mats will form on the surface of the water. Chlorine will kill the algae, but, the geosmin will travel thru the distribution system. Water systems nationwide that have this problem are looking towards removal of the algae from the lakes or streams. The use of air to stir up the water is one method of controlling the growth and spread of algae, sonic waves or other devices have been developed recently to help curb the growth, chemical sprays is another way, though not one that is desirable. Along a similar path recent findings have established that molds found in streams and discharges of wastewater plants produce toxins (mycotoxins) of stream samples taken a majority were shown to have several different mycotoxins in lower amounts. Usually in PPT's or parts per trillion. While levels as high as 1mg/l. (1 milligram per liter)was found in wastewater treatment discharges. Now where this would come into play is when you have a sewage treatment plant directly upstream from a water treatment plant water intake.

Some of the detected mycotoxins found were:

Deoxynivalenol; found in most of the samples taken

Nivalenol; second most widely found

Beauvericin; third highest reported in the samples taken

Three others (zearalenone, a-zearalenol and B-zearalenol) are what is referred to as estrogenic compounds.

Care in the treatment of raw waters to a water plant is a must as water is being bottled for use by mothers in the preparing of baby formula.

The last microorganisms I wish to touch on are the viruses. These are smaller than bacteria, and cause diarrhea, vomiting and cramps as well.

Plus Ultraviolet light does not work well on these critters; reason also why EPA does not accept it as a primary disinfectant. In recent years some strains of viruses have been found that will kill you. So far mostly they have been found in other countries, not here in the United States. And facilities like the CDC (Center for Disease Control) have been at the forefront of studies into just how serious a threat these viruses might be.

The last two things I want to touch on in this chapter, is one how chlorine fits in here. Chlorine has been found to be the best true defense against these organisms, and is the reason why EPA and States will not ban its use in water treatment. And second is Turbidity, and its effect on drinking water and the disinfection process. Turbidity is a measure of cloudiness in water, suspended particles, that can help disease causing organisms get past the disinfection process. Ultraviolet light must have water free of turbidity to be able to get at the microorganisms. Another reason EPA and States do not accept Ultraviolet light as primary disinfection.

Now if you happen to use a well for your private water supply. And thinking of using ultraviolet light to kill bacteria; place two water filters before the light the first filter should catch particles 5 microns or larger. The second one, closest to the light should be able to catch particles 1 micron in size. And don't forget to keep the glass tube clean of dust and dirt. Any dust or dirt on the tube will keep the light from passing through the tube, allowing any bacteria to get past.

Chapter Four

I now want to talk about chemical contaminants, and how they affect us. I will start with what are called the Inorganics, many of which are naturally occurring. The first one is Antimony, MCL of .006 milligrams per liter {mg/L}. Can cause a decrease in blood sugar, and is found in ceramics, fire retardants and from petroleum refineries. Have not seen an positive results for Antimony from any water system I have ever dealt with.

Next is Arsenic, a big deal was made of this a couple of years back, when the White House wanted to cut back on the limit reductions for this. The MCL is .010 mg/L, Arsenic can cause cancer, skin damage and circulatory problems. And can be found thru erosion of natural deposits, runoff from glass plants, or from fruit orchard runoff.

Asbestos, this element is read not as an MCL but in million fibers per liter. In drinking water the risk is not to the lungs, but to the intestines. Where polyps can form you need to check with a doctor on this. Asbestos can be found from erosion of natural deposits or by decay of asbestos/cement lined water mains, though this is very rare.

Barium, this element has an MCL of 2 mg/L and can cause high blood pressure. And can be found thru erosion of natural deposits, discharge from metal refineries and drilling operations.

Beryllium, has an MCL of .004 mg/L, and can cause intestinal lesions. This element can found from metal refinery discharges, coal burning plants and discharges from electrical, aerospace and defense industries.

Cadmium, has an MCL of .005 mg/L and can cause kidney damage. Found naturally in the ground erosion is a cause as well as in paints, batteries and corrosion of galvanized pipes.

Chromium, has an MCL OF 0.1, and can cause skin problems. Erosion of natural deposits, and discharges from steel plants and pulp mills are the sources.

Copper, copper is one of two with an action level {Lead is the other}. The action level for copper is 1.3 mg/L, depending on exposure, as to the illness potential of copper. Ranging from gastrointestinal illness to liver or kidney damage. Corrosion of household plumbing due to aggressive water is one problem. Erosion of natural deposits is the other problem associated with copper.

Cyanide, has an MCL of 0.2 mg/L and can cause nerve damage or thyroid problems. Sources of this element are discharges from steel factories, plastic and fertilizer plants.

Fluoride, has an MCL of 4 mg/L can cause mottled teeth in kids and bone disease in adults. Found as a natural element, Dentists recommend some levels of fluoride usually not more than 1.2 mg/l be applied to children's teeth to help fight tooth decay. There are public water systems which add controlled levels of flouride to their finished water. When I was working as a regulator I would get calls from dentists asking for a list of water systems which added fluoride to their water supply. Any system that did add fluoride were made to sample for it on a regular basis.

Now I want to turn attention to the issue of Lead in drinking water. Like copper, lead has an action level of 0.015 mg/L, and accumulates in body tissue, as previously noted in this book. Years ago lead was used in water pipes and in solder, and is known as a soft metal. A metal which was dissolved easily by aggressive waters, waters of a PH of 7.0 or lower. Early in the development of the Safe Drinking Water Act the EPA and the states developed regulations for both lead and copper in drinking water. Water systems, which had any old lead lines were encouraged to replace them and the sale or use of lead solder, was banned by law. Homeowners were warned about the use of lead solder on in home plumbing, though, no law could force a person from using lead solder in their home. Water systems which might have had some old lead lines in their systems, found that by boosting PH and Alkalinity levels up. A coating would form inside the pipes thus the water was in an nonabrasive state and no lead or copper would leach off the pipes. Today, the problems associated with both lead and copper in drinking water is nearly nonexistent. Chalk one up for the EPA and states, in removing one problem element from our water supplies.

Now another very bad element found on earth, Mercury, has caused some problems to our water supplies over the years. Known for causing Kidney damage, mercury can be found thru erosion of natural deposits. Or as a byproduct from factories and refineries, landfill runoff and runoff from croplands. A very potent inorganic, mercury has an MCL of .002 mg/L. Mercury is one of the standards in Inorganic sampling, thru many states. And like lead and copper, mercury will buildup in the body tissue until damage occurs.

The next two on our inorganic list is Nitrate and Nitrite, both derivatives of Nitrogen. Both can be found as natural deposits, as well as ingredients in fertilizers. Both, when found, can be tell tale signs of sewage contamination. Mothers should avoid giving infants water with high levels of either. As serious illness or even death might occur, also known as Blue-Baby syndrome. The MCL for nitrates is 10 mg/L, while, only 1 mg/L for nitrites. It was determined that water systems that use chlorine would not need to sample for nitrites, as the chlorine would eliminate the nitrite in water.

Another inorganic Selenium, has an MCL of .05 mg/L. Selenium can be found naturally, but is also associated with petroleum refineries, or discharges from mining operations. Medical concerns associated with selenium are: Hair or fingernail loss, numbness in fingers and toes, and circulatory problems. In my years as an inspector, I have not found selenium to be a problem, as all sample results I viewed were below the MCL. That was in my small area of Western Pennsylvania, and may not be the case in other parts of the country.

Last on the inorganic list is Thallium. With an MCL value of .002 mg/L. thallium can be found in discharges from glass, drug or electronics factories. Medical problems associated with this element are hair loss, changes in blood; liver, kidney or intestinal problems. And like Selenium, I have not seen results above the MCL levels set by EPA.

Chapter Five

In this chapter I will turn my attention to the Organic compounds. We associate them in two groups the first are the Volatile Organic Compounds or VOC's. For sampling purposes, we have twenty such compounds. Should a water system get a hit on any one of those, then, a twenty first Vinyl Chloride is also requested. In the next chapter, we will talk about the other group, the Synthetic Organic Compounds, or SOC's. Of which the EPA adds to this list, every few years, with additions due on a five year basis I believe. Lastly I will talk about Disinfection By-products, their health effects, and their relationships to disinfection agents.

There are twenty-one VOC's listed, {in Pennsylvania} twenty are sampled for and the twenty-first Vinyl chloride is sampled only if a hit is detected in any of the others. For the most part VOC's are cancer causing, but some can cause other illnesses. The list is as follows:

Benzene: Has an MCL value of .005 mg/L, and can cause cancer. Has been found in some foods, gasoline, drugs, paints plastics, and pesticides. Granular Activated Carbon {GAC}, will remove benzene from water. Sampling for this as with all VOC's is done in the distribution system, after treatment.

Carbon tetrachloride: Has an MCL of .005 mg/L, aand is also a cancer causing compound. Has been found in solvents, and their degraded products. As with all VOC's, GAC is a method of removal from water.

Chlorobenzene: Has an MCL of .10 mg/L, and is linked to liver and nervous system disorders. Chlorobenzene is a product of waste solvents in metal degreasing.

A quick note before I continue, when you see a Bi or Di in the name of the compound. Or numbers such as 1,1,1 or 1,2,1 these are referring to the number of atoms of a chemical {as in the Bi or Di} or the bonds between atoms {as in the 1,1,1}.

o-Dichlorbenzene: Has an MCL of .60 mg/L, and can cause liver, kidney, or blood cell damage. This compound can be found in solvents, paints, engine cleaners, dyes, and chemical wastes. p-Dichlorobenzene: Has an MCL of .075 mg/L, and is a known cancer causing agent. This is found in room and water deodorants, as well as in "mothballs".

1,2—Dichloroethane: Has an MCL of .005 mg/L, and will cause cancer. This is found in leaded gasoline, fumigants, and paint.

Cis-1,2-Dichloroethylene: Has an MCL of .070 mg/L, will cause liver, kidney and nervous system problems. It is normally found in industrial solvents.

Trans-1,2,-Dichloroethylene: Has an MCL of.10 mg/L, and will cause liver, kidney and nervous system problems as well. And is also found in industrial solvents.

1,1-Dichloroethylene: With a MCL value of .007 mg?L, is known to cause cancer, as well as liver and kidney problems.

It can be found in perfumes, plastics, dyes, and paint. But people, don't worry about using perfume, no evidence has been found to cause alarm. Just do not drink the perfume.

1,2-Dichloropropane: MCL value is .005 mg/L, can cause cancer, and liver or kidney damage. This is found in soil fumigants and industrial solvents. Heavy rains can wash this into rivers or lakes and be picked up by water plant intakes.

Ethyl benzene: has an MCL of .70 mg/L, and can cause liver, kidney and nervous system problems. This one is found in gasoline, insecticides, and chemical plant wastes.

Dichloromethane: With an MCL of .005 mg/L, this one is a cancer causing agent. It is found inpaint strippers, metal degreasers, and propellants.

Styrene: Has an MCL of .10 mg/L, and can cause liver or nervous system damage. This is found in plastics, rubber, resins, and as waste from drug plants. Styrene has been found to leech out from city landfills.

Tetrachloroethylene: Has an MCL of .005 mg/L, and will cause cancer. This is found in dry cleaning and other solvents, so be careful on disposing of these items.

Toluene: Has an MCL of 1.0 mg/L, and can lead to liver, kidney and nervous system disorders. It is an additive in gasoline, and is found in many solvents.

1,2,4-Trichlorobenzene: This has an MCL of .070 mg/L, and will cause liver or kidney damage. It is found in herbicides and in dyes.

1,1,1-Trichloroethane: The MCL is .20 mg/L, affects both the liver and kidneys, and the nervous system. This compound can be found in adhesives, aerosols, textiles, paints, inks, and metal degreasers.

1,1,2-Trichloroethane: With an MCL of .005 mg/L, this form of dichloromethane will also damage liver, kidneys and the nervous system. It is found in rubber compounds, other organic products, and chemical plant wastes

Trichloroethylene {also known as trichloroethylene}: Has an MCL of .005 mg/L, and will cause cancer. This is found in textiles, adhesives, and metal degreasers.

Vinyl chloride: Has an MCL of .002 mg/L, this one is only sampled for when another one of the VOC's has been detected. Vinyl chloride is a cancer causing agent. It is formed when solvents breakdown, and may be found leaching from PVC pipe.

Xylenes: This group has an MCL of 10. Mg/L, and will also cause liver, kidney, and nervous system problems. Xylenes are found as a by-product of gasoline refining, in paints, inks, and detergents.

Chapter Six

Now I will focus on the SOC's, or Synthetic Organic Compounds. The largest group by far, SOC's are your herbicides, pesticides, dioxin and others. How these become a problem is that they wash into our rivers, lakes and streams from rain events. I will, as I did with the VOC's list each with its MCL. At the end of this chapter I will list the names as you might see them in stores.

Alachlor—Has an MCL of .002 mg/L, and is known to can cancer. It is widely used in pesticides, so far it has not been a problem in drinking water supplies.

Atrazine—Has an MCL of .003 mg/L, and has been found to cause birth defects in rats. This compound is found in herbicides, and new studies have been done on atrazine. EPA and the states are targeting this chemical and some levels have been found in raw water tests. People with wells need to avoid using this around their wells. As it can leech down into the groundwater.

Benzo(a)pyrene—Has an MCL of .0002 mg/L is noted as a cancer causing agent. Found in cigarette smoke, and on charbroiled meats. It is found in the coal tar and in road sealants. I have not seen a case of any hits in drinking water associated with this compound.

Carbofuran—The MCL for this is .04 mg/L, and can cause damage to the nervous system and reproductive system. It is found in many pesticides on the store shelves today. There have been studies done on workers exposed to this compound. With many cases of nervous system problems noted. I have not seen any hits of this compound in any sample results during my time.

Chlordane—Has an MCL of .002 mg/L and is cancer causing. Found in pesticides used at one time to kill termites around homes. This compound has been pulled from shelves years ago. I did have an experience with chlordane once. A small community in Greene County Pennsylvania, had used this around many of the homes. We were called into investigate, as all the homes were on wells and some health issues had come up. We went in as a team and pulled samples from as many houses as we could, finding some hits, if I remember right. Well a few years later, a public water line came thru the area, the people connected to the line. I have never seen an hit for this on any sample result over the years.

Dalapon—The MCL for this is .2 mg/L, and can cause liver and kidney damage. Used as an herbicide to control weeds around crops and drainage ditches. It is around drainage ditches that concerns the EPA and states, as it may wash into rivers, or lakes. I have not found any hits associated with this over my time as a regulator.

Di(2-ethylhexyl)adipate—With an MCL of .4 mg/L, may cause liver and damage to testes in people. Found in synthetic rubber and food packaging materials. It becomes a problem when it leeches out from waste dumps.

These last three chapters contain a lot of technical data that might be somewhat hard to understand. When you go to a hardware store for a container of weed killer or a bug killer. Take the time to read the label then refer back to this book to see what could happen when you ingest some in the water you drink. The same goes for the auto parts store that sells motor oil, antifreeze or the various motor additives you might put in your cars engine. Maybe you will be a bit more careful in handling these liquids in the future and not just flush them down a drain or down a storm sewer. All this adds to the problems faced by your local water plant operator. Plus helps to drive up their costs for treatment; which adds some to your water bill. And nobody likes higher bills; one tends to get upset when we see our utility bills increase. Well in the case of our water bills, we can be part of the blame.

When reading these chapters don't get hung up on the numbers associated with the various chemical compounds. This book is not intended to be technical, but for the average person to gain some knowledge of what is out there. If you have a quest for further knowledge, a chemist could shed light on the various compounds and what the numbers mean. My intention is to show you that when you see one of these compounds. You will understand just what could happen to you if you ingest it.

Chapter Seven

A hot topic these days is what the researchers refer to as Endocrine Disruptors. Which are varied, anything from Plastics in baby bottles, to pesticides, to most recently pharmaceuticals, such as steroids, human growth hormones (HGH), estrogen pills, or testosterone.

The endocrine system in our bodies produces chemicals which help maintain body functions, and are referred to as glands. What researchers have found is that chemicals imparted into our drinking waters from these items, interfere with the normal workings of our glands. You might ask, how can this happen? Well, when a normal healthy person ingests these chemicals, thru their tap water, these chemicals begin to work on the body's endocrine system. A normally healthy person would not knowingly ingest these medications.

Now lets take a closer look at one part of this issue that has just come to the forefront in recent years, Pharmaceuticals. These are the medications prescribed by your doctor, such as Steroids, or HGH (human growth hormones). Also listed is Nitroglycerin, which is used by some people with heart problems. Researchers are also looking at over the counter medications such as aspirin, ibuprofen and acetaminophen. Other pharmaceuticals, such as tranquilizers, depressants, antibiotics have been found in water. The hormonal chemicals given to beef cattle to increase growth, found in our watersheds.

You might ask how these were discovered. Well a few years back researchers had found fish that had both female and male reproductive organs in them. This led to a study on our water supplies on the issue of pharmaceuticals in our waters and how they got there. Oh, you people who enjoy your bottled or vended water your also at risk here.

Such medication as Estrogen, ladies, finds its way into our water supplies. Now you want to know how this happens. Whenever a doctor prescribes a medication, you take it, some gets absorbed in the body some passes out as waste. This waste goes to the sewage treatment, which is not capable of removing such waste. Treated waters then are discharged back into our rivers, lakes, and streams, picked up by water treatment plants downstream. The water treatment plants in turn, cannot remove these chemicals from the water under normal treatment procedures. Let us not forget all the unused pills we dump down our toilets. These medications also end up at the sewage plants. To date only Reverse Osmosis has been found to effectively remove these chemicals from water. Recently, many communities have taken to setting up collection points for unused medications. These meds are then properly disposed of, check with your local communities to see if such a program is set up.

In the case of farm animals, their waste is deposited onto the fields and pastures of our farmlands. Well a good rain washes these chemicals into our rivers, lakes, and streams.

Now you might ask how this can affect our health. Well there is the growing question of women who are pregnant, drinking water with these pharmaceuticals. Researchers look at possible problems in embryo development, human blood cells and in cancer cell development.

These chemicals referred to as endocrine disruptors are the medications and enhancement drugs given to livestock. Another form of endocrine disruptors is the insecticides used to halt growth or reproduction in insects. If they affect the insect's ability to reproduce, what will they do to us?

So what can we do to stop these items from entering our water supplies? Well, one way is to use our medications until they are finished. That way there is nothing to flush down commodes. Another way is to place any and all unused medications in sealed containers and get them to an approved landfill. I have given some thought to burning these chemicals. A super intense heat could be a solution to this growing problem.

Chapter Eight

The issue of terrorists attacking our water supplies is very real. A few years back terrorists were captured with plans to attack our drinking water supplies. How can they do this and how can we stop them? This question I will answer by explaining first how and why. Then what measures we can take to stop them and protect our families and ourselves.

Why anyone would want to attack our supplies is simple, one attack could wipeout thousands of people and the perpetrators could get away almost undetected. One such way is by the use of high pressure hose to force feed lethal contaminates into the water lines. Done from the distribution system, this would be indictable until people start dropping over dead. To stop this, systems would need to install proper backflow prevention devices at the meter. This will cause contaminates to flow into the ground thus ending the problem. Another method of attacking our finished water supplies is to feed contaminates into a finished water storage tank. Both by climbing the tank, opening the hatch on top and dumping the item in. Or by drilling a hole in the overflow pipe and using a high pressure hose to force feed contaminates. To prevent this, systems need to place the tank ladders high enough so that another ladder would be needed to reach it. Air gaps in the overflow pipe will stop anything being fed into the pipe. Surveillance equipment and double fences would help keep unwanted people out as well. Alarms placed at remote locations can alert authorities to unwanted entry. A timely response would be needed to end the situation. Coordinated drills between water, police and fire officials can cut down on response time. We as citizens living near booster stations or storage tanks can do our part by alerting police or water company people to break-ins.

An attack to the raw water/water treatment system is harder to do. Contaminants placed into the raw water supply can be removed either in the treatment or disinfection processes. There are a couple of microbes though, that can be introduced and make it thru normal disinfection. These organisms would need to be mass produced and fed into the clearwell. These organisms are in a sheath that prevents normal doses of chlorine from killing the organism. In the case of Clostridium Botchelium, it is not the organism but the toxin produced that can harm us. Another threat one less likely would be a direct attack takeover of a water plant. If in control a terrorist could feed contaminants as they wish. Or implant enough nuclear material to render the plant unusable. By cutting off the electrical supply we can stop contaminates from entering the system.

With most water treatment plants handling surface water, this would be harder to do surveillance equipment detecting entry and the use of cell phones can alert police to a problem. Some systems that use ground water wells or spring water for a supply could have other issues. A well, or spring could be miles away from the treatment plant thus out of site of plant operators. An intruder could feed contaminates into the well, unseen. If the system does not have the same type of treatment as a surface water plant there can be problems. All water systems should be made to adhere to the same treatment schemes to prevent attacks on the raw water supplies. The use of reverse osmosis systems can help keep out unwanted contaminates. The only drawback would be the waste of water in the form of brine. Usually it takes ten gallons of raw water to produce four gallons of finished water. The other six gallons in the form of brine would contain any contaminates. Another issue a terrorist would look at is size and location of a system. Does the system feed a hundred people or a million? Is the system located in a large city, or in a rural town? In any case how many other systems are fed by a plant? Do neighboring communities buy their water from the target system? If so this can add to the death toll, these community leaders need to be informed of any situation. What kind of response can we expect? Local police, state police, National Guard, or FBI. In any issue of terrorist attack the FBI and Homeland Security would be notified and take charge. Even so what kind of response time are we looking at? Five minutes, five hours? time is critical in these matters to stop the threat. Now if we are looking at a spring water supply, who owns the surrounding land above the spring site? And what type of treatment does the spring have? In the case of land ownership, anyone who owns property above the spring opening can drill a well into the aquifer supplying the spring. Thus injecting contaminates into the supply. Now the type of aquifer could determine how far some contaminates can travel. A limestone aquifer compared to a sand aquifer where the sand could act as a filter. The limestone could be more porous. All public water systems in the state of Pennsylvania provide disinfection to kill off microbial contaminates. It's the chemical contaminates that disinfection does not affect. Other additives in the treatment process are used on non microbial contaminates. For wells and springs proper detection methods would include the drilling of monitoring wells upstream of the well or spring housing. At these sites electron probes that signal contamination would be used. While a terrorist could disable a probe, an alarm would alert workers to a problem. And as with storage tanks, a well can be fenced off.

I just mentioned fencing of vital areas around a public water system. Lets look at the various types of fencing design and how this could act as a deterrent. The best fence to use would be a high chain link fence with barbed wire across the top. Now while we see that chain links can be cut, alarms could be placed to go off once a link is cut. Thus alerting authorities to the threat, response time is critical here. An intruder would be working as fast as possible. So how do we slow them up enough until the Calvary arrives?

It has been said recently that to contaminate a public water supply, it would take a huge amount of contaminate to have any real affect to the citizen base which draw water from a system. The old adage the solution to pollution is dilution is very true. But to say, an attack on our water supplies is impossible, is a bit miss leading. Highly improbable, for sure, but I find almost nothing is 100% true. And it is for this reason that a person should get to know their local water supplier. And know just where the various tanks or booster stations are in your area. Should you see anyone trying to climb a fence or break into a water treatment building, call both the water company and then the nearest police station. No matter whom the intruder might be, it is a crime and should not be taken lightly. In this age of terrorist attacks, we are forced to be more watchful and mindful that this is the very water we use to drink, cook and bathe in. An open line of communication exists between the water supplier, and law enforcement; federal, state and local. And with newer measures of protecting these systems the respond times are shorter. But it still takes our observing and making the quick call to set these wheels in motion.

Let's look at each component of a typical public water system.

Let's start with the water treatment plant. Most of which are large buildings, with some land surrounding. Look at the farthest points and build double or even triple barbed wire fence totally surrounding the plant if possible. Motion detectors and cameras can alert staff to unwanted visitors. If the plant does not operate 24/7 then have the detection equipment monitored by police. Work with the authorities to develop the quickest possible response time. As in all such cases the authorities need to come armed with backup. But let's say, someone does get past this deterrent. The next step would be to have windows barred or with very thick panes. And doors should be thick steel designed. With built in sensors that alert authorities to a break in. Having a security force on sight with call in instructions could help as well. And for surface water plants lets not forget the intake. Should it be a lake, river or even the oceans? The same rules for fencing apply here as well. Cameras observing the waters around the intake can alert authorities to potential dangers. Intakes should be sealed off if possible and diving should be prohibited. But with any river or lake this could be impossible as a diver could enter the water in areas unseen by plant employees. The next area of concern would be the filters. After sedimentation or flocculation chambers the water passes thru the filters. Some contaminates could be introduced here and make it thru to the clearwell. Most Microbial contaminates though would be killed off by the disinfection process. While chemical contaminates could make it thru to the distribution system. A terrorist could mask a drum of contaminate as a treatment chemical to escape detection. A daily check of in use chemicals by the operator might catch this and switching containers can correct this. After the filters, the next area of concern would be the clearwells. The clearwell is the first area of finished water. The disinfection process usually starts here. The clearwell is found in ground, after the filters, or under them. Using locked hatches with alarms should the hatch be opened would help. But once the hatch is opened, anything could be tossed in and make it out into the distribution system.

Chapter Nine

Now I want to devote a chapter to the distribution system. I will explain what makes up this part of the water supply, what can happen here, and how to make this part safe. The distribution system is made up of: water line; storage tanks; booster stations; and fire hydrants.

The water lines: pipes in ground usually six inches in diameter or larger. This would be the strongest link in the chain. Placed in ground four feet or more deep, large equipment would be needed to dig down to the lines, making it almost impossible for an attack.

Storage tanks: there are several types of tanks used in a system, some of which help provide added pressure to the system. First type I want to talk about is the ground tank. This tank is built from the ground up, with a hatch on top and a caged ladder along the side to climb up. Hatches should be locked and ladders placed high off the ground to stop an attacker from climbing up to the hatch. These tanks also have an overflow pipe attached to prevent overfilling. Placing a large air gap high up in the pipe would prevent anyone from feeding contaminants under pressure up the pipe. Water suppliers should not place sampling taps at lower levels in the tank. Anyone can feed anything into the tanks under pressure here. Place any sample taps a good fifteen to twenty feet off the ground, so only employees with ladders can reach them to draw samples. Usually there is a valve pit in ground where shutoff valves are placed to shutdown the tank. This would help isolate any contaminates that might have been placed in the tank.

The next type of tank, the in ground tank is built underground. This tank is close to the surface and is easier to attack, usually, with a cement pad on top where the hatch would be placed for access. Anyone could dig down or drill into the hatch and easily drop in contaminates. Placing a good alarm system and proper response times are needed here, as this would be a weak link. Many in ground tanks have an overflow pipe that would be easy to get to; care is needed with these tanks. Suppliers should shy away from using in ground tanks, for security reasons.

The next tank a system might use is called a standpipe, which is a tall skinny tank used to add pressure in areas where a pressure boost is needed. Standpipes provide storage plus pressure to the system. As with ground level tanks, hatches need to be locked, ladders placed high off the ground, any overflow pipes air gaped.

Lastly, I want to talk about elevated tanks. These tanks sit high off the ground, on legs. Elevated tanks usually have an enclosed middle where valves, piping, and ladders are heavy steel doors, locked, bar entry to the ladder and valves. But once entered provide concealment for any intruder to do damage. Again proper alarm systems with quick response times are needed to prevent someone from contaminating the tank.

As with any part of a system, proper fencing and alarm systems need to be provided to keep this part safe. Double fencing with sensors is a must especially if the tanks are located in rural areas.

Now I will explain booster stations, what they are, and what is needed to do for protection of the supply. A booster station is used to add pressure to the water, thus aiding in providing water to customers who are in higher elevations. Some booster stations have sampling taps or are used to feed some chemicals into the system if need be. The buildings used to house the stations usually have steel doors, some have windows. The best ones are windowless and have thick steel doors to make entry harder by an intruder. Even so, high fencing, (double preferred) with sensors and alarms are needed. Hopefully there will be quick response times, as this could be a weak link in the system. Many water suppliers today use a computerized system to monitor all aspects of their supply, both at the plant and in the distribution system. An operator can check tank levels, or tell which valves are opened or closed, or remotely open or close a valve. Steps are being taken to safeguard these computer systems to prevent hackers from breaking into the network and disrupt operations.

Now the weakest part in this chain, the fire hydrant, poses problems from the standpoint of both sheer numbers, and that they are not fenced off. While special wrenches are used to open the cap and valve that allows water to flow. Others can get these wrenches to open the hydrant enough to feed contaminates into the distribution system. One saving grace, is that most hydrants are in highly populated areas, thus in plain sight of people. If you live near a hydrant, get to know the employees of your system. If you see someone working a hydrant you do not know call your water supplier. Hydrants are also used by water suppliers to clean out distribution lines. Sometimes gunk will build up in dead ends from old cast iron pipes that might still be a part of the system. When you turn on your tap and see brown water, well this is what you're seeing. Some iron bacteria has been known to grow in these lines, call your supplier and let them know.

In areas where there were a lot of private wells, a good water supplier will make sure these private wells are taken off line before a new customer is added to their system. Anytime you have private wells tied into a public system without proper backflow preventers, contamination can occur. Anyone wanting to attack a supply, could feed a contaminate into the well then pipe that bad water into the public supply. Opening a nearby hydrant could cause what is referred to a back siphoning or backflow. Customers downstream of the site would be in danger when they turn on their taps.

Everything I have discussed in this book has been looked at by the states and the EPA. Professional organizations such as the American Waterworks Association or AWWA, were formed to pass along information and provide training to water systems who are members. Each state has a chapter and hold meetings where information is discussed and training provided. Get to know your water supplier and the agencies who work to protect your water supply. And if you live by a plant, a tank, a station, keep your eyes open. Should you see a problem call them.

Chapter Ten

In this chapter I want to look at the potential dangers that could come about by a terrorist attack on a bottled water plant. A lot of the water bottlers today use camera systems in their plants to oversee production. While this is a great tool to avoid problems, it is not fool proof. The bottling companies need to background check all employees and future hires. Could an employee sneak a vial small enough to avoid detection? And be positioned at a point where they could slip in a poison? Once these bottles are filled and packaged, then shipped. Now the contaminant is out where the public can buy it. As explained earlier if the contaminant is chemical, disinfection will not have an effect. For bottlers who produce the large five gallon cooler bottles. The containers are returnable, who is employed to smell or use a probe to detect contaminants? Who oversees washing of the containers prior to filling? It would be easy for a terrorist working in these areas to slip a poison into containers. Once these five gallon containers are capped and palletized they are shipped to dealers. At the dealers, they are stored in warehouses and delivered to homes. The dealers do not have the security systems to keep a constant watch over the supply. What would keep a terrorist from say using a needle to inject a poison into a container?

One good thing in tracking down the problem is that bottling companies keep records of each batch of water processed. Lot numbers are assigned and kept on record. These records would show dates produced, sometimes times as well. Another reason to secure these plants from attack is that our military purchases bottled water for our troops. I was conducting an inspection a bottling plant one day when an inspector from the military was there. I must say though, we both could have missed a terrorist with a vial. So how can we better protect these supplies? Well changing people around from time to time would help. Along with constant supervision by trusted staff who will stay on top of things. Even down to storing of the packaged supply, constant watch is needed. Any employees, who exhibit irrational behavior, place in less sensitive areas of operation, or placed on leave, or even terminated. The dealers who handle the large containers need to install camera systems and equipment to detect break-ins. Alerting authorities when a break-in happens. Thus if someone tries to contaminate any containers, they can be pulled. Pulled they can be analyzed and kept away from the customer. This could start with through background checks when hiring employees. Have new employees drug tested and criminal background checked. During hours of operation have supervisory staff on the floor at several points in the process. To keep watch, know your employees, and their habits. If the bottler uses a well on the premises make sure the well is closed off from the general public. It should be fenced and cameras positioned to keep an eye on the supply.

Chapter Eleven

The future of our public drinking water supplies lies in a national communications network system. I feel that the federal government thru either the EPA, or Homeland Security, or both needs to take charge. There needs to be a link up of every state or regional network now in existence. And if there are areas not currently networked then new networks need to be formed. The current systems have the feds providing funds to states. But each state can only spend the money in their state. For example, money given to Pennsylvania cannot be used to fund projects in West Virginia. By having each EPA region administer funds over their region. Proper networking can be put in place. The next step in the process would be the formation of a national computer website to link all state's networks. Information can be passed along from state to state or region to region. A national board of directors would be formed to set up policy and procedure.

The board should be made up of water people from each region of the country, plus representatives from the EPA; Homeland Security; The US Coast Guard and one state out of each region. Drills should be set up and run at various times to test proficiency of each individual network. And by drills I mean on a quarterly basis, with active participation from all involved. Police, water companies, coast guard and FBI. Which results could be passed along nationally. The leadership of the board should be hand picked amongst the members and should change after terms expire. Each state will be able to input their thoughts and ideas. When a state comes up with new technology, members could attend training seminars from the various regions to enhance their own network systems. The goal is to keep everyone on the same path to drinking water security. Water is our most vital asset that we depend upon to survive. I ask you the public; take a greater interest in the water that you drink. No matter if it is out of the tap, a bottle or a cooler. And don't forget the ice you buy and use for drinks that is water too. All that I have talked about on drinking water applies with our ice plants as well. Contaminated water can become contaminated ice. Releasing the poison as the ice melts in the glass. Sometimes one can detect an odor to the ice/water. Or a cloudy appearance, that could lead one to question the safety of that cube of ice. If you buy a bag of ice and you find that there are dark spots imbedded in some of the cubes. Or that cubes have a dark color, these could be warning signs of potential problems. Do not discard the ice, keep it frozen. Contact the state agency that regulates and give the bag to them. Make sure you tell them where you bought the ice. The regulatory people will need to trace back to the company that made the ice. And see that all bags in the shipped lot are pulled from shelves. The same would also be followed in the case of a possible contaminated bottle of drinking water as well. Bottlers should have records of their shipments and where each pallet of water bottles is shipped.

IN CONCLUSION:

Everything I have put down in these pages has come from over 27 years of work in the field of drinking water regulation. From the eyes of the people whose job it is to protect and safeguard the very waters that we drink, and bathe in. And while some might denounce the use of say chlorine to disinfect the very waters we use. What you are not told is how little chlorine is actually added. Nor are you told about the actual amounts that is put into the water. When you see the symbols PPM or PPB those refer to parts per million or parts per billion. And the very reason that chlorine is used, it can readily be traced so we know that it is there doing what it is intended to do. That is kill off harmful microorganisms so as to keep you and your family from harm. There are other methods to disinfect water, but, these are not easily traceable. Don't you want to know that when you shower, when you take a glass of water from the tap, when you get a glass of water from that cooler, stop at a water fountain at a mall or store, or buy a case of bottled water and open one up that you are consuming the safest water you will find. Or that the bag of ice you just bought to put in your drinks is free of contaminates.

When you look at where the majority of your drinking water comes from. Mainly, a river, lake, or stream, and of recent even the oceans, sources that are open to possible contamination from a variety of sources. Sources that are either natural or man made. Yet because of the strict nature of the federal safe drinking water act. With the civil penalties that can come down on the many suppliers both private and public. Time and a great expense is put forth to keep the quality of the water you drink safe and wholesome.

Oh and lets not forget our groundwater supplies. While deep underground and not normally as susceptible to contaminates. They too must be sampled and sometimes treated like surface waters. Wells must be kept sealed so no surface water can get in. Springs are the hardest because here is where the groundwater meets the surface. Greater care is used to make sure the springs are protected from any possible contamination from above ground. When you buy a gallon of spring water, it has come from a spring developed for your safety. Sealed from exposure to the elements and bottled in plants those not only sample the water being bottled. But also inspect the bottles being filled for shipment to stores all over the land. Get to know your local water treatment plant, get to know the inspectors who visit the plant and keep tabs on each plant. In some states one can visit the offices where inspectional records are kept. And look at the reports to see just how good a job your water company is doing.

In the pages of this book I tried to show, the kind of contaminates we are faced with. And what harm could come to a person. As well as the possibilities of terrorism, however so slight to our treatment facilities. Of which I tend to disagree with the theory put forth that it cannot be done. Water is the very building block of life itself, and needs to be both respected and protected.

Acknowledgements

I wish to acknowledge the EPA's list of contaminates for much of the information for this book, as well as the states who helped by providing sampling needed to develop the standards we use today.

Also the work of the USGS, whose sampling and reports have helped to contribute much knowledge and understanding for both the regulators and the water suppliers.

Thanks to:

Barry Herr, Pa. D.E.P. Whom I picked up some supervisory skills from.

Prentiss Watkins, City of Houston, Tx. Drinking Water Operations, a very bright water person who knows her job better than most.

Mark & Terri Turner, City of Houston, Tx. Drinking Water Operations, great coworkers I had the pleasure to work with.

Gene Wolbert, Pa. D.E.P. A very smart supervisor I had the pleasure to work for.

The E.P.A. For coming up with the Safe Drinking Water Act regulations.

Pa. D.E.P. For giving me the employment to write this book.

George Senoct, former supervisor for PADEP

Ron Bargiel, water quality manager for PA American water company

CPSIA information can be obtained at www.ICGtesting.com
Printed in the USA
LVOW07s2249310316

481608LV00002BA/349/P